Memorable Graces

Testimonies, memories, anecdotes, and
favors granted through the intercession of
Blessed Father Solanus Casey, O.F.M. Cap.

Richard G. Beemer with Linda Leist

Memorable Graces

Testimonies, memories, anecdotes, and
favors granted through the intercession of
Blessed Father Solanus Casey, O.F.M. Cap.

Richard G. Beemer with Linda Leist

Memorable Graces

Testimonies, memories, anecdotes, and
favors granted through the intercession of
Blessed Father Solanus Casey, O.F.M. Cap.

Lambing Press

Lambing Press
Pittsburgh, PA
www.lambingpress.com

ISBN 978-1-950607-17-4

Cover art by Jacob Flores-Popčak.
Inside pages by Araceli Chavez.

Printed in the United States of America

DEDICATION

To all of those who are devoted to
Blessed Father Solanus Casey
and to all of the faithful who contributed
to the making of this little book.

CONTENTS

ACKNOWLEDGEMENTS

As many an author has noted, it takes a great number of people to publish a book from conception to finally making it into print. In keeping with that tradition, I would like specially to thank my dear friend Linda Leist, who worked tirelessly and spent copious hours seeking out and interviewing many of the book's contributors. Thank you and God bless you, Linda, for your devotion to this little book; friend Father Tony Steinacker, pastor of Sts. Peter and Paul Church, Huntington, Indiana, for promoting the developing book at the conclusion of Mass and for his offer to publish the book if I couldn't find an interested Catholic publishing house; dear longtime faithful friend of many years David Scott, vice chancellor for communications for the Archdiocese of Los Angeles, for connecting me with Mike Aquilina's publishing company, Lambing Press, located in Pittsburgh; friend Hannah Swenson, daughter of the aforementioned Mr. Scott, who graciously volunteered to input into her computer all of the handwritten stories I received and email them back to me in a very timely manner; friend Danny Bickel, who along with the stories he contributed, also wrote about a wonderful holy relic of Blessed Solanus Casey that was gifted to Sts. Peter and Paul Church by an anonymous donor; friend Jan Scher, for her devoted work, suggestions, encouragement, and prayers; friend Father Edward Foley, O.F.M. Cap., vice postulator for the canonization cause of Blessed Solanus Casey, who clearly explained in his Foreword to this book that "remembering, storytelling, letter writing, and public testimonies of ordinary believers" contributes greatly, and "as the final journey toward his canonization continues, these tales continue to be extremely important"; friend Debra Kriegbaum, for her efforts to see to it that announcements to acquire stories appeared in parish bulletins throughout the Fort Wayne-South Bend Diocese; friend Paul Siegfried, who contributed a Prologue outlining Blessed Solanus' journey; the Huntington County TAB newspaper, which granted me permission to reprint an article concerning Blessed Solanus' induction into the 2021 class of Huntington County Honors; to our parish bulletin editor, Amy Wilcox, who graciously published many reminders for parishioners to contribute their stories; and finally, to all of those who were compelled to contribute to this little book. If I've missed anyone, please forgive me. God bless all of you! ❖

INTRODUCTION

I never had the pleasure of knowing Father Solanus Casey, O.F.M. Cap., during the time he lived at St. Felix Friary in Huntington, Indiana, from 1946 to 1956. I was born in 1950, eventually the oldest of eight children. When I was five years old in 1955, my mother decided it was time to expose me to the holy Mass at a different location, particularly the early Sunday Mass at the friary, which, looking back, seemed to me to be a very early Mass. However, she loved the Capuchins, and wished to be in their presence whenever she could.

Being only a few years out of diapers, I had no understanding of the Mass, of course. But I do remember some of the sights and sounds I experienced. The image that stands out the brightest in my memory is of the friars, processing quietly one by one in their dark brown robes into the chapel to their melodic recitation of Gregorian Chant, which immediately caught my attention. Something else I didn't understand. I'm sure the saintly Father Solanus was among them, blending in with the prayerful procession of friars. The sounds of chant, however, did stay with me forever, and may have contributed to my love of listening to and playing music from a young age.

Fast forward to 1963. I was thirteen, and I asked a friend of mine, Ken Brennan, to hike with me to the friary for a visit. He agreed. I lived on the southern border of Huntington's city limits, he lived on the northside, and the friary was located on the far western and northern limits of the city.

It was a Saturday, I believe, when I left home to trek the distance to my friend's home and then on to the friary. The reality of city life abruptly ended beyond the gravel road in front of St. Felix. North of the gravel road as well as to the west and a bit to the east, there were no homes, no other urban growth, no bypass, nothing but miles and miles of fields planted in corn, beans, wheat, and alfalfa. The friary then was quietly and peacefully isolated.

We were a little tired, parched, and sunburnt when we neared the friary on the dusty Flaxmill Road to the friary. Finally on its premises, we walked up the steps to the building and rang the doorbell, or perhaps we knocked. A young, friendly brother, Brother Francis Mary Sparacino, the porter, greeted us and escorted us in, and who I learned from Vice-Postulator Father Ed Foley that the porter died in 2015, not very long ago. Brother Francis surmised immediately that we were probably thirsty and offered each of us a cold can of soda.

We thanked him and asked if he could show us around the inside of the friary and around its grounds. I don't recall the order of the sites we took in, but I remember large rooms, one of which contained a mountain of non-alcoholic beverages, another large room where they made their clothes, and another that I believe was the bakery, smelling of fresh-baked bread. The rest of the interior of the friary escapes my memory, but the grounds were beautiful and carefully manicured.

All of this is reminiscent, and over time my memories of the friary may have succumbed to embellishment and cloudy remembrances, but I remember the sights, sounds, and smells of the friary from long ago and have kept them with me during my lifetime. I am grateful for those memories, and I "Thank God ahead of time" for them. God bless Blessed Father Solanus Casey, O.F.M. Cap.! ❖

— *Richard G. Beemer*

Editor's Note: To learn about the Catholic Church's process for the making of saints, visit the website of the United States Conference of Catholic Bishops, USCCB.org/saints.

FOREWORD

It is an overstatement to suggest that stories make saints. All of the legends about St. Patrick driving out snakes or taking on the Druids did not cause him to be such a fierce and commanding missionary. Nor did all of those tales about St. Francis preaching to the birds or taming the wolf of Gubbio turn him into God's troubadour and one of the most beloved figures in Western Christianity. Even more pointedly, the invention of the genre we know as the Gospel did not produce Jesus' divinity or create his unfathomable union with God. Stories do not make saints, nor do they produce holiness.

On the other hand, stories are critical vehicles for revealing the journey to holiness of the Church's Blesseds and Saints and endearing them to believers who wish to emulate their sanctity. Even more to the point, tales of Servants of God and those the Church calls Venerable are required elements for recognizing and establishing their virtues and even miraculous powers. Although stories do not make saints, they certainly help the faithful and even the official Church to recognize saints.

The power of narrative in the beatification and now canonization process for Blessed Father Solanus Casey is undeniable. This is especially true of the memories and tales, reports, and anecdotes of ordinary folk that have been collected over the decades since his death in 1957. These narrative gifts — whether simple tales of Solanus' kindness or awesome reports of healings — were the undeniable fuel that fanned the flames of devotion and fired the cause for his beatification.

While his brother Capuchins celebrated his sanctity, and multiple religious superiors and bishops inside and outside the Franciscan family were aware of his extraordinary gifts of healing and consolation, they were not the impetus for opening a cause for sainthood on his behalf. Rather, it was the tens of thousands who came to pay their last respects at his death, who joined the Father Solanus Casey Guild, and submitted official and unofficial reports of the many ways he touched their lives.

Without the remembering, storytelling, letter writing, and public testimonies of ordinary believers, the process toward his beatification would never have had such power and have come to such a blessed conclusion.

As the final journey toward his canonization continues, these tales continue to be extremely important. Thus, this modest collection of memories and gratitude, especially from Father Solanus' years at St. Felix Friary in Huntington, Indiana (1946-1956), broaden the palette of tales already recorded and published. They are like new rows of flowers planted in the ever-expanding garden of reminiscences and memorable graces that grow in the fertile soil of Blessed Solanus' legacy.

In gratitude for these freshly collected testimonies, we pray that they nourish the growing devotion to "God's Porter" and allow the grace of his canonization to blossom in due time. ❖

— *Father Edward Foley, Capuchin, Vice Postulator, the Canonization Cause of Blessed Solanus Casey, Detroit, Michigan.*

PROLOGUE

'Faithful to the present moment'

On Nov. 18, 2017, more than 60,000 people filled Detroit's Ford Field, a crowd normally reserved for professional football games or huge concerts.

On that day, however, those attending were there to witness a special ceremony honoring a simple, humble man of God who had spent his life among the poor and the infirm.

Mary Lou Snyder's photo of a glowing Father Solanus, photographed at Sts. Peter and Paul Church in Huntingtin, Ind., in 2023.

The beatification of Father Solanus Casey bestowed upon him the title of "Blessed," the final step before sainthood, which would possibly make Father Solanus the first American-born Catholic male saint. Among those in Detroit to witness the rite were faithful from Huntington County, where Father Solanus had lived for ten years late in his life, and where there were many accounts of his healing hand and inspiring counsel.

Huntington was just one ministry stop in the life of the man born Bernard Francis Casey on Nov. 25, 1870, on a farm in Oak Grove, Wisconsin. Known as Barney, he was the sixth of sixteen children born to a devout Catholic family of Irish immigrants.

When he was eight years old, a wave of diphtheria spread through the Casey family. Two of his siblings died. Barney survived, but his voice was permanently impaired. As a young man, he worked a series of odd jobs, including lumberjack, hospital orderly, and prison guard. It was while working as a streetcar operator that he witnessed the brutal murder of a woman by a drunken sailor. The event affected him deeply and led to his call to become a priest.

He enrolled in seminary in Milwaukee, but with little formal education, he struggled with academics. He was advised that his best path to priesthood would be to join a religious order, where he could become a "simplex" priest with limited duties.

Casey heard a call that he should go to Detroit, where he joined the Capuchin order. It was there he was given the religious name "Solanus" after St. Francis Solanus, a 17th-century Spanish Franciscan with whom he shared a love of the violin. He made first vows on July 21, 1898, and was ordained on July 24, 1904. He celebrated his first Mass a week later in Appleton, Wisconsin, with his family in attendance.

For the next twenty years, Father Solanus was assigned to parishes in New York City, where he was sought after as an inspirational speaker, and became known for his healings of the sick. By 1924, he was back in Detroit at St. Bonaventure Monastery, where he helped found the Capuchin Soup Kitchen, which was instrumental in serving the local population during the Depression. His main ministry was that of a simple porter, or doorkeeper, but thousands visited expressly to meet him.

His health began to fail, and in 1946 he was sent to St. Felix Friary in Huntington to recover, but his reputation for lending comfort and a healing presence preceded him, and many pilgrims traveled to Huntington to see Father Solanus. He lived in a small room and slept on a simple straw mattress, and never turned away a visitor or anyone seeking his counsel. He always seemed to have just the right words of comfort for everyone who knocked on his door.

Among his most famous words were: "We must be faithful to the present moment or we will frustrate the plan of God for our lives."

In 1956, Father Solanus returned to Detroit. In the last year of his life, he became close to a young brother Capuchin, Father Ron Rieder. The two shared a love of music. With Father Ron playing the organ at Mass, Father Solanus would stand next to him and sing, even though his injured wispy voice left him a terrible singer. Father Ron would sit and listen to Father Solanus play his cherished violin.

Later, Father Ron was assigned to Sts. Peter and Paul Church in Huntington, where he was a beloved religious leader himself over many years, inspired by his time with the dying priest. Father Solanus died on July 31, 1957, with his final words, "I give my soul to Jesus Christ." More than 20,000 people viewed his coffin prior to his funeral and burial.

The cause of his beatification began in 1976, even though many of his personal papers and records were lost following his death. An initial inquiry by the Catholic Church confirmed upon Father Solanus the title of "Venerable" by Pope John Paul II in 1995.

The next step toward sainthood involves the Church's approval of a miracle.

The case for Father Solanus was confirmed in 2017, and approved by Pope Francis on May 4, 2017, leading to his elevation to the title "Blessed" at the beatification rite in November of that year at Ford Field in Detroit.

Father Rieder was instrumental in the creation of a memorial to his fellow Capuchin in Huntington. The St. Felix Friary, which had changed ownership in the time since Father Solanus' residence, was purchased by Fort Wayne philanthropist John Tippmann in 2009. The aging building was renovated and reopened as the St. Felix Catholic Center.

The spartan room in the friary where Father Solanus lived for a decade was also restored and remains a shrine for visitors and pilgrims. An outdoor statue of Father Solanus was added in 2018.

The Huntington community has remained connected with Father Solanus over the decades. A Huntington extension of the Father Solanus Guild was created in 2012. Another Huntington group, Praying with Father Solanus, holds monthly Masses for the sick where parishioners may receive a blessing from an icon of Father Solanus. The group is also working to build a St. Joseph's Prayer Walk on the St. Felix property. ❖

— Paul Siegfried is a member of the board of directors of Huntington County Honors, which was created in 2014. Huntington County Honors highlights

both the famous and those who are less well known. Candidates must have made a lasting impact on Huntington County or brought recognition to the community through their actions or achievements in one of five categories: athletics and recreation, business and professional, community and public service, humanities and cultural, and historical.

Once a friend, always a friend

By Danny Lee Bickel

Danny Bickel

Dad had many friends, and among them was Father Solanus Casey, a member of the Franciscan Friars, a Capuchin Order of St. Francis, residing at St. Felix Friary on Flaxmill Road. Father Solanus was sent to Huntington in 1946 to retire and spend his remaining years in peace and solitude.

Many favors were attributed to Father Solanus, and although he was supposed to be retired, many still came to ask his advice and to find a sense of spirituality. The presence of Father Solanus soon spread throughout the community. Dad was no different than all the other faithful who wanted to meet this saintly priest. Father Solanus never refused to see anyone, no matter the time of day or night, or how exhausted he might be.

Dad was very impressed with Father Solanus for his wisdom in matters of family and religion. I'm sure Father Solanus was equally impressed with dad's faith in God and his devoted love for his wife and family of eighteen children. I remember going with dad on one of his visits. One thing that really stuck in my mind was the relic that Father Solanus carried in his robe. Encased in a small, round glass container was a small splinter from the cross of Jesus. He held the splinter to my face and said that I could kiss it. As I did, I should say "Thank you, Jesus." When he spoke to you, he made you feel you were the most important person in his life. And in that moment perhaps you were.

During their conversations, dad found out that Father Solanus had never driven a car. Dad was driving a green 1949 Chevy and talked Father into taking a driving lesson. They proceeded to the friary's parking lot, where dad explained the gear shift, clutch, brake, and gas pedal. Father Solanus popped the clutch as he gave the Chevy some gas — too much gas! As they rounded the parking lot, dad was frantically trying to gain control of the steering wheel as they clipped the bushes that surrounded the outer edge of the parking lot. Father Solanus let off the gas as dad reached over and turned off the key in the ignition. Getting out of the car, Father Solanus said that was his first and last driving lesson. I don't know who was more relieved, dad or Father Solanus.

A sketch of Father Solanus Casey, by Danny Bickel.

My sister Pam had a large growth develop on her neck. There was concern that the growth might be cancer. Dad took her to see Father Solanus to seek his blessing and to check out her ailment. He touched my sister's neck and said, "Take her home. She will be all right." He didn't say take her home and pray to God that she will be all right. He said, "Take her home. She will be all right." This was a blessing God had bestowed upon him: Jesus working through the body of a frail old priest. It wasn't Father Solanus healing my sister, but through his intercession, Jesus allowed the healing to take place.

One day mom asked my brother Jim (Butch) to take my little sister Pam down to the park. Erie Park was less than a block away. While at the park, Pam climbed up the slide. She admired her big brother Bob, who was a fireman, and she knew he slid down a pole at the fire station. Wanting to imitate him, she leaned over the edge of the slide, grabbed a support

Norbert "Fritz" and Garnet Bickel with their daughter Pam at her first holy Communion.

pole, wrapped her legs around it and started to slide down the pole. She dropped much faster than she had anticipated. Later on, she told me she didn't remember hitting the ground. The last thing she remembered was seeing the big steel plate at the bottom of the pole.

The next thing she remembered was waking up and Butch helping her to her feet. The large growth on her neck had broken open. Butch took his bleeding sister home. Mom took her to Dr. Brubaker, and to his surprise,

2

the growth had disappeared. He put several stitches in her neck to close the opening. It was just as Father Solanus had told my dad earlier, when he said, "She will be all right."

During the several years that Father Solanus spent in Huntington, the friendship between him and my dad grew closer and closer. They had an agreement. The first one to die would throw a rope down from heaven and pull the other one up. On July 31, 1957, Father Solanus was the first to die, so it was his responsibility to lower the rope for dad when it was his time.

Norbert "Fritz" and Garnet Bickel

Dad was stricken with Parkinson's disease, a crippling disease affecting muscles and the nervous system. Dad had Parkinson's for more than ten years and it confined him to bed for several more. Being confined as he was, he developed bed sores, his neck became so weak that he was unable to keep his neck up. In order to shave him, his head had to be physically raised to shave under his chin and neck area. Not able to use his feet, they were no longer at a ninety-degree angle, rather closer to a forty-five-degree angle.

On June 4, 1976, dad died as his children and family members gathered around his bed. Just before he died, he opened his eyes that had been closed for several days. He turned his head and looked around the room, using neck muscles that hadn't been used in years. He then looked up and gently passed away. One of my sisters said, "Did you see dad? He looked at all of us, as if to say goodbye." Someone else said, "Before death you have a burst of energy and all your senses are elevated, allowing dad to open his eyes and move his neck."

Faith is believing, and in believing God can do many things that we as humans cannot fully comprehend. I believe dad was looking around to find the rope being lowered for Jesus to receive his soul. At that moment he felt a presence of Jesus and his friend, Father Solanus Casey. ❖

From the self-published book "A Little of This ... A Little of That ... And a Whole Lot of Other Things," by Danny Lee Bickel. The book is a collection of memories of growing up in a family of twenty in Huntington, Indiana. It can be purchased at the Huntington County Historical Museum, 315 Court St., Huntington, IN 46750. The cost is $10.

• • •

The relic that touched lives

Father Solanus Casey was no stranger to the Bickel family. Father Solanus and my dad, Norbert "Fritz" Bickel, had much in common. Both came from a large family. Father Solanus was one of sixteen, and dad had eighteen of his own.

Their conversations pertaining to family life were very similar. Both families led lives, let's say, of not being rich. But both families were rich in another way: rich in faith. The Bickel family grew up praying the rosary every evening, on or about 7 p.m. After our evening meal and the dishes were washed, no one was allowed to go on a date, play with friends, or go anywhere until the rosary was prayed. It only took a short while to pray the rosary, so our schedules were adjusted for that period of time.

The front and back of a popular second-class relic of Blessed Father Solanus Casey.

Often, our Protestant friends would sit and listen while we recited the rosary. I'm sure Father Solanus' family had a similar dedication to the rosary.

I was only three years old when Father Solanus came to Huntington in 1946. I had the privilege of meeting him, as he and my dad were friends. Not often, but once in a while, he would come to our house for an evening meal. He felt right at home with the many kids running about.

A friend of ours, Vicki Thompson, asked for the help of Father Solanus on a couple of occasions. Vicki's father, John Ness, had a heart transplant, so Vicki knew she may have heart problems in her lifetime. In June of 2007, Vicki had a heart attack. It was questionable whether she would survive. Her husband, Paul, requested my second-class relic of Father Solanus, which was made from a piece of the robe Father Solanus wore when he was alive. I worked with Paul and had told him about an experience my daughter's friend had with the relic.

My daughter Danielle and her husband, Harold, had moved to Jackson, Tennessee, due to a job change. They became very close friends with a couple in their neighborhood, Kevin and Laurie Bryant. They were having trouble carrying her pregnancies full-term. Laurie had three miscarriages and was pregnant again.

I asked Danielle if Laurie would wear my Father Solanus relic, and although Laurie was not Catholic, she agreed to wear it. With many prayers and the intercession of Father Solanus, Laurie went full-term and gave birth to a healthy little girl. That was twenty years ago. Since then, Laurie has given birth to two more healthy children.

Paul knew that Father Solanus had helped many, and he wanted his help for his wife. She completely recovered, and both were very grateful for Father Solanus' intercession.

In 2009, Vicki was diagnosed with cancer. She started chemotherapy treatment and found out she was allergic to it. Again, it was a serious situation, and again Paul asked if he could borrow my relic. She wore the relic, and with many more prayers and the intercession of Father Solanus a second time, Vicki recovered and has been cancer free ever since.

We took Father Tony Steinacker, pastor of Sts. Peter and Paul Church in Huntington, to the hospital to give Vicki the anointing of the sick. Vicki told me later that she was afraid she was going to die, but after the anointing of the sick and her wearing of the relic, she felt at peace and was no longer afraid.

Although my relic is frayed and worn, I carry it with me always, for I don't know where or when someone will need the help of Father Solanus Casey. ❖

The restorative power of prayer

By Mike Perkins

Mike Perkins

Though I consider myself a nominally devout Protestant, I have had a very personal bond with Blessed Solanus Casey for more than a quarter-century.

Here is how it began.

Through the late spring and early summer of 1995, at the age of 47, I was not feeling well. I had contracted a respiratory virus in February and had never quite shaken it. My energy was flagging. I had a constant, dry cough, which interfered with my sleep. I was always short of breath, especially after even the slightest exertion.

One June evening, breathing had become so difficult I got into my car and drove around the city, with the air-conditioning on full blast, the dashboard louvers tilted toward my face in an effort to force air up my nose. I knew then I needed help. The next day, I went to the emergency room at the local hospital. Several tests and a chest x-ray later, I was diagnosed with bronchitis, given a prescription, and sent home. Later that day, a physician friend of mine happened to look at my x-ray and saw something he didn't like. He had me admitted directly to a hospital in Fort Wayne. The next day I was told I had a condition called idiopathic (unknown origin) cardiomyopathy and that I was in congestive heart failure.

I was even more shocked to learn that the medical endgame for cardiomyopathy was a heart transplant. Depending on how I responded to treatment, that might be my final recourse. My cardiologist said "about three percent" of people with this condition regain normal heart function. I knew my life would be different — and likely much shorter — from that point on.

I was home from the hospital a few days later. As word of my condition spread, visitors would stop by the house to cheer me up. Among them was a lady named Joan McClure. My wife and I had gotten to know Joan at our United Methodist church. She had recently converted to Catholicism.

She brought her best wishes for my recovery and left something with me.

As she said goodbye that day, she pressed some hope into my hand. It was a relic of Father Solanus Casey, widely available to the faithful, consisting of two small plastic ovals bound in yarn. Encased between the ovals is his photo on one side and on the other side, his last words and a tiny snippet of cloth that had been touched to his tomb. I knew a bit about Father Solanus from local lore; he'd spent some of the final years of his life in the community where I live and was widely admired. Joan told me to keep the memento with me whenever I could. When I assured her I would put it in my wallet, because that's the one thing I always carried, she had one admonition: "Just don't let it touch any money."

I followed her instructions and tucked it away in an inner compartment of my wallet. I was grateful for the kind gesture and the prayers from Joan and others that came with it.

And, from that day forward, I got better.

Over the next few months, I adapted to my medications and exercise regimen. I began breathing normally again and regained my energy. My measurable heart function returned with astonishing speed. My doctor was impressed. My wife and children were delighted. I was awed by what I assumed was my good fortune, and by what I am convinced was the restorative power of prayer. Many people were praying for my recovery. Often, I would pull the relic from my wallet, and spend a few moments to ponder Father Solanus' visage and the dark scrap of cloth. I came to understand there was much more working on my behalf than the medicines and the daily walks.

I am certain that God, through Father Solanus, has provided me with a special healing. I don't presume to know how it works, but what I do know is that I am one of the few people with idiopathic cardiomyopathy who have recovered full heart function and have had a chance to enjoy a normal life.

Thanks to my friend Joan McClure, Father Solanus is with me today, and I will keep him with me every day for the rest of my life. I don't know why I deserve his blessing, but I believe that I have received it, and I thank God for it. ❖

'The pain was absolutely gone'

By John Francis McCullough

I had torn my rotary cuff in my right shoulder while lifting a heavy bag of weeds and dirt at Marmion Abbey in Aurora, Illinois, on June 13, 2017. I was landscaping the grounds by the sanctuary outside for Deacon Antony Marie to prepare them for the arrival of Bishop David Malloy of the Diocese of Rockford, Illinois, who was coming to officiate at an ordination.

John Francis McCullough

I took the 60-pound bag of weeds and dirt to the dumpster behind the abbey. As I lifted the lid on the dumpster, I must have thought I was Samson and threw the heavy bag with my right arm and heard four pops, which tore the cartilage in my shoulder. I knew I was in trouble, and I was in excruciating pain, so I went looking for Deacon Antony for a prayer. After the ordination I drove back to Huntington, Indiana, still in pain that would last for three years. I couldn't lift my arm up past my shoulders, and I realized I had done something I should never have done.

On a side note, two weeks after the ordination I tore the left shoulder. The tongue of the wheelbarrow I was pushing up a trailer ramp got stuck because I was going too fast. I iced my shoulders every day for three years, and after three years I had finally had enough. I went to Sts. Peter and Paul Church in Huntington, and after Mass I approached Father Tony Steinacker, the pastor, and asked him to just touch my right arm with the ciborium. He turned with the ciborium of hosts in his hands and touched my shoulder with it along with saying a prayer and asking for an intercession from Father Solanus Casey to heal me. I had an immediate healing on that March 13, and I could lift my arms above my shoulders. The pain was absolutely gone. So, I left Father and went home with the feeling that it was healed.

I told Father Tony I was healed and thanked him many times for the healing. I had a doctor's appointment on June 13, 2020, to follow up and get a medical opinion. I was excited to tell him I was healed, so he examined it for the miracle. The doctor confirmed that something took place. As far as movement, the arm was one hundred percent. They sent all the documentation to Bishop Kevin Rhoades of the Diocese of Fort Wayne-South Bend, and to my abbot, Abbot John Brahill, O.S.B. I never heard back. ❖

The dream of a better life with Jesus

By Troy Szelis

The following is from an essay written by the son of Mary A. (Shaffer) Szelis, on her 75th birthday (2014). Mary had a personal account involving Father Solanus Casey.

Mary Szelis

The encountering of people and the capturing of one's attention reminds me of my mom's story of how she met Father Solanus Casey in the 1940s on her grandma's (Sophia Ludwig) farm. Mom recollects that when she was around seven years old, Father Solanus was visiting farms in the area.

It was clear that Father Solanus played a big part with inspiring my mom. Father Solanus was her dreamcatcher of a better world for mom. As she recalled, she would see the priest and a few local priests coming down grandma's long lane a few times during her summer stays at grandma's.

Grandma Sophia's house sat near the present-day Norwood's Nursing Home off old U.S. 24 in Huntington, Indiana. Mom climbed on top of the chicken coop so she could be unseen and listen to what the priests were talking about. Because of her loving and ornery nature, she would make comments on top of the roof just for the fun of it. She would calmly say, with clarity, "It's going to rain."

She would add noises to get a rise from these holy visitors. Father Solanus and the priests would stop along the path, astonished by what they had heard. From atop the chicken coop, my mom would add more and more noises, "egging" them on. Suddenly, one of the priests said, "Maybe we should get home out of the rain?" They questioned one another about "the voice" they had heard.

The priests said between them, "I think God is in the woods; do you think so?" "Maybe he is in the field?" They would even look at the chickens to see if God was revealing himself through poultry. This "foul" prank was hilarious to mom. She could not stop laughing, as her silliness and the priest's comments continued.

As they moved on, she climbed off the roof and made her way from the back of the coop to meet up with Father Solanus and the other priests. She wanted to hear what else they were saying. My mom asked the visitors why they walked near the chicken coop. They said, "God talks to us at the chicken coop." Mom nearly lost it with laughter.

Grandma Sophie heard the priests exclaim, "Your place is haunted!" Grandma said, "No way! This place is not haunted!" She added a further defense by saying, "I have not heard from a ghost yet!" Mom laughs to this day about the voices she made that day.

On a more serious note, on one of these walks to grandma's house, Father Solanus was suddenly struck with a strong pressure in his side. He stopped instantly and gasped as if he had lost his breath. His priestly escorts asked in surprise, "What is wrong with you?" Father Solanus said, "God poked me in the side. Do you know why?" He thought a little while, and then he insisted that God was telling him to say something to this little girl he had met.

His long white beard glistened with the summer's sunshine as he looked at my mom and revealed his prophetic message for her: "Little girl, God told me that you will go far in life!" Mom was captured in the vision of Father Solanus as she was to us. Father Solanus was being used as an instrument of God to capture the dream/vision for my mom. The same can be said of my mom using the Holy Spirit to lead her to catch the dreams and hopes of people she encountered. Father Solanus and mom were passing along the message that the dream of a better life can be found in Jesus. ❖

A short life made longer with love

Susan Iannucilli as told to Linda Leist

Dolores Ann "Laurie" Kohrman, who was born on July 8, 1935, in Fort Wayne, Indiana, broke her right leg around the age of sixteen. It was set in a cast to mend. When the cast came off, the doctors found it had not healed. She had developed cancer in her leg below her knee. They removed her leg above the knee to remove all the cancer.

Eventually, she developed new sites of cancer in her left leg and her right arm bones. These were removed, too. Her mother, Lucille, went to Huntington to the friary where Father Solanus was living because she had heard of how some people had recovered from their illnesses after visiting him.

She knocked on the door and he answered it. She asked if he could pray for Laurie. He looked up at the sky and stared for a while as if he was listening to something. He finally turned back to Lucille and told her, "I think she will surprise the doctors." Lucille went back home.

The doctors said Laurie would not live very long with the cancer. However, she lived miraculously for about five more years. In this extra time of her life, she lived happily with her family and enjoyed several new nieces and nephews. She talked often with parish priests and had great conversations about Jesus.

She was right-handed before her surgeries but was willing to use her left hand to do many things. She painted beautiful oil paintings, which she gave to family members. She would ride around in her wheelchair, pushing herself with her one good arm. When I was two years old, I remember her scooping me up onto her lap from her wheelchair and giving me a ride. It was good fun! Her cousins would take her out to the lake and take her into the water for some fun. Laurie didn't seem to let the bad things get her down.

Laurie died on Aug. 31, 1956, at the age of 21. It seems that, with the help of Father Solanus — by praying to God — Laurie had extra time to enjoy this world, and her family enjoyed her being with them longer, too! ❖

An old man in a brown robe

By Father Ron Rieder, O.F.M. Cap.

Father Ron Rieder, O.F.M. Cap., former pastor of Sts. Peter and Paul Church, Huntington, Indiana.

I received a phone call: "Father, we are not Catholic, and are an old couple. Could you come to see us?

"Last night, my husband slept in a chair in the front room — he has cancer and sleeps in the chair, I am in the bed in the bedroom. I heard this talking and thought he had the radio on.

"The next morning, I went to the kitchen and found two piles of pecan shells on the table. My husband said, 'You'll never believe this, but last night I couldn't sleep and all of a sudden there was an old man in a brown robe standing in front of me. He said he was hungry, so we went to the kitchen. I found a bag of pecans and he ate them. He said God sent him to prepare me for death, that he would come to help me when I die.' He was so confused. I had a picture of Solanus and showed it to him. He said, 'That's the man who was here last night.' "

I never saw these people after that. But Father Solanus loved Huntington. ❖

• • •

We as a couple of novices weren't feeling well and went to Father Solanus' room and asked for prayer. He said, "No, Capuchins are supposed to suffer." ❖

• • •

A man fell, injuring himself very seriously. I went to the hospital to visit him, and he was in real bad condition. I pinned a Father Solanus badge on his bed. He made a complete recovery. ❖

A man was dying of cancer, and he was in a coma. He was non-Catholic. His wife, a parishioner, asked me to bless him. He had no visitors, and I pinned a Father Solanus badge to his bed. He made a complete recovery. This happened more than 24-30 years ago. He still works full time in a very prominent job. ❖

I was scrubbing toilets as a novice and felt sorry for myself. All of my high school graduate classmates are at Notre Dame, etc. Here I am on my hands and knees in a monastery scrubbing toilets. Father Solanus walked into the bathroom and said, "Oh how lucky you are to be cleaning toilets for your brothers!" I thought he was crazy, but I never forgot those words. He lived that way. ❖

Risky surgery was her only hope

Jerome B. Kearns as told to Linda Leist

Her name was Angela "Angie" Krouse. Her parents were Richard and Lois Krouse. She was born in Fort Wayne in 1954 with a hole in her heart. That was not her only birth ailment but the most severe and critical.

She was examined by multiple doctors in and around Fort Wayne. Each one advised her parents that the hole would not allow her to live more than a few months and that a highly risky surgery would be her only hope.

Open heart surgery in 1954 was unheard of, particularly with an infant and, therefore, chances of survival were very low, but without it her chances of living more than a couple of months were zero. My aunt and uncle had heard of Father Solanus and his ministry to the sick and visited him in Huntington several times.

On the last visit, Father Solanus told them that Angie would not require surgery and that she would live a happy life. They subsequently had her examined again by her pediatric cardiologist, who found the hole in her heart was no longer there. She lived to be 42 and died in 1996 of other complications. ❖

Simultaneous life-threatening situations

Kenny Eckert as told to Linda Leist

Kenny Eckert, of Huntington, recalled the story he heard from his mother, Emma Eckert, many times. Two of Kenny's older brothers, Don and Chas, were in life-threatening situations simultaneously.

Don was serving in the military during the Korean conflict. Our mother often heard disturbing stories on the news, and consequently, she feared for her son's life.

His younger brother, Chas, was injured in a very serious car accident. He was a high school student at that time. After remaining comatose for two weeks, doctors didn't expect Chas to ever recover. They gave the family no hope. It was 1952 and medical technology offered no more answers.

Emma, a woman of great faith, went to see Father Solanus, asking intercessory prayers for both of her sons. The very next day, after praying with Father Solanus, her comatose son somehow awakened from the coma, fairly jumped out of bed, as she recalled, and doctors could never explain his sudden and complete recovery!

Emma recounted to her son Kenny that on that special day of prayer, Father Solanus had assured her that Chas would be fine.

Emma also stated that she had made several appointments to pray with Father Solanus, and her sons both survived these life-threatening situations, she believed, due to the powerful intercession of a gentle, holy priest, Father Solanus Casey. ❖

The gentle holiness of Father Solanus Casey

Courtney Weigman as told to Linda Leist

Wyatt Schmaltz was a normal, healthy baby boy at birth, the youngest of three sons of April and Joe Schmaltz, then at age three (2014), he was diagnosed with neuroblastoma, the second most common childhood cancer, with characteristic tumors.

His parents took him for treatment at Lutheran Hospital in Fort Wayne, Indiana, and Riley's Children's Hospital in Indianapolis, Indiana. He underwent chemo, radiation, and a clinical trial medication procedure in New York City. Wyatt nearly died because of the immunotherapy, and a code blue was called.

The medical team revived him, and two days later, on Sept. 19, 2018, he was released, as medical personnel had exhausted their resources.

The sacrament of the anointing of the sick was requested, with the intercession of Father Solanus Casey. Father Tony Steinacker, pastor of Sts. Peter and Paul Church in Huntington, administered this sacrament to Wyatt, giving him spiritual strength and God's grace through the Holy Spirit.

Father Tony stated that whenever he gives the anointing of the sick, it is through the intercession of Father Solanus. Many of us agree, as his gentle holiness is as powerful in heaven as it was on earth.

Eight days after Wyatt was anointed, he went for a cancer scan on Nov. 15, 2018. The doctor was amazed to report that the scan results looked good, there was nothing to report, and deemed Wyatt to be in remission.

For several months, Wyatt was able to play baseball, then had the port removed, with no activity restrictions. He was able to lead a normal childhood, enjoying family and friends.

However, he was still being monitored with regular scans, per protocol.

In May of 2019, a collection of cancer cells was detected in his right arm. He was again prescribed chemotherapy, but to no avail.

He passed away on July 24, 2020.

Still, we ask ourselves, is it simply "coincidence" that eight days after Wyatt was given the anointing of the sick, with the intercession of Father Solanus, prayerfully requested by Father Tony, that scans revealed no cancer cells and Wyatt was in remission?

Or isn't it possible the intercession of Father Solanus is the decisive element that enabled Wyatt to enjoy some carefree timelessness, experiencing his childhood days, making memories with his family and friends? ❖

A sanctuary friary

Carol Bucher, widow of David Bucher, as told to Linda Leist

David Bucher, age fourteen, lived in a basement house with his dad and brother on Hitzfield Street, just south of the apple orchard, then part of the monastery, St. Felix Friary (now St. Felix Catholic Center).

A cousin was babysitting David and his brother, and she was accompanied by her son, who was older than the two boys.

This older boy started arguing with the two brothers. Aware of the older boy's escalating anger, David ran outside, barefooted, to avoid potential physical violence. He ran through the apple orchard toward the back door of the monastery. Apparently, Father Solanus had seen David running through the snow, opened the door and invited David in. He provided David with food and wrapped him in a dry blanket, listened to his story, and consoled him with his prayer and blessing.

Later, after the kindly old priest walked him home, David knew that he would never forget the kindness, consolation, and love he received that night from Father Solanus Casey. ❖

The making of miracles

By Linda Leist

Linda Leist

I am Linda Scher Leist, second cousin of Jan Scher. I have known her for many years, and since my retirement a few years ago, I have been privileged to know her better. Her unwavering faith and trust in God and his perfect plans are two strong attributes I see in her.

So, when I was notified of her car wreck on May 22, 2019, I went straight to Lutheran Hospital in Fort Wayne, Indiana, to offer prayers and support. I often carry a Father Solanus badge in my pocket, and fortunately I had it with me to hold on to while praying for her. Our friend, Jackie, joined me in prayer at the hospital, as we prayed for the intercession of Father Solanus to restore Jan's health. She herself had a Father Solanus badge pinned to her hospital gown, also invoking his intercession.

Three times that afternoon, the doctor, Jan's orthopedic surgeon, came to the surgical waiting area and informed us that they were unable to proceed with the surgery to pin her arm back together because her blood gases were very unstable, and they couldn't safely give her a general anesthetic to put her under because her carbon dioxide (CO_2) level was extremely high, and her oxygen (O_2) level was extremely low. After trying for hours to stabilize her blood gases (CO_2 and O_2), a different option was agreed upon. Instead of a general, a local anesthetic was used for the surgical procedure, so Jan was awake, praying during her surgery.

Hypercarbia, where not enough oxygen enters the lungs, and a concurrent deficit of the emission of carbon dioxide, seemed to be a major medical concern, as this imbalance can cause shortness of breath, confusion, lack of consciousness, respiratory failure, and death. Arrhythmias may also occur if the heart and brain are lacking oxygen and have excessive levels of carbon dioxide.

Using only a local anesthetic, the bones of Jan's forearm were pinned together, and the doctor explained that the surgical staff was uncertain if Jan could fully regain consciousness under a general anesthetic, due to her compromised respiratory system.

After a few long hours the doctor updated us. The grim facial expression he wore wasn't what I was hoping for, as he informed Jackie and me that Jan's arm would heal well with physical therapy, but then he looked me straight in the eyes and said, "But her arm isn't her problem."

I said, "Oh, what is?" He replied that it was her lungs, as her carbon dioxide level was still extremely high. I said, "Oh no, isn't there something you can do?" With steady eye contact, he informed me, "No, there isn't anything more we can do."

I stared at him, waiting for words of hope, but he didn't give me any. He said, "She is very sick," and then he left. I turned to Jackie, and she looked just as shocked and sick as I felt. We continued to pray.

Jan Scher

Jan's medical history starts on June 26, 1947, on the day of her birth. She was diagnosed a "blue baby," a term used to indicate babies who lacked oxygen at birth. According to Jan's mother, at the time she was born, medical staff struggled to get Jan to take her first breath.

The doctors told the parents that Jan probably wouldn't live long, maybe just two years or so, because the oxygen transport system wouldn't function properly. She wouldn't grow up normally, due to her compromised respiratory system.

However, her parents' strong faith led them to take her to what was then known as St. Felix Friary, home of Father Solanus Casey in Huntington, Indiana, who had been accredited with many divine favors after interceding with Our Lord for many people.

According to her parents' report, Father Solanus blessed their newborn baby, prayed for her, and told them Jan would be OK. Her parents took her home and loved her. They also took her and her five siblings to Sunday Mass at St. Felix Friary throughout Jan's childhood.

Her spiritual friendship with Father Solanus was, and is, ongoing throughout her life.

At age two, her parents decided to have Jan evaluated at Riley Children's Hospital in Indianapolis, Indiana. The pediatric staff could offer no solutions in the medical world, but her parents trusted for answers in the spiritual world through the intercession of Father Solanus.

Jan stated that at the age of 36, she consulted with a doctor, an orthopedic surgeon in Fort Wayne, Indiana, to research her prognosis. She had been born with a small body frame, diminished lung capacity, and shortened neck length. He ordered x-rays, then later called her in to explain his conclusion. He told her that when he displayed her body x-ray, he couldn't figure out how she walked through the office door, saying, "If I didn't see you walking through that door, I'd say your x-ray belonged to someone who would not ever walk."

Jan was informed that if she ever contracted pneumonia or broke her neck, it would be lethal in her situation due to her birth defects. You guessed it. She once broke her neck at c2-c3 and also contracted pneumonia at one time. We think Father Solanus has been really busy with Jan. She said she feels as if Father Solanus is always with her, caring for her in many health situations.

The pediatric staff at Riley Hospital invited Jan's parents to bring her back periodically for checkups, but they chose to totally trust in Our Lord with the intercession of Father Solanus in imitation of his humble, sincere spirituality. Jackie and I found ourselves doing the same thing after Jan's surgery and discouraging news from Dr. Hicks.

We continued praying until late that night, when staff informed us that Jan's blood gases were stabilizing and they would keep her on a bi-pap oxygen machine throughout the night and continue to monitor her.

Her respiratory system was stabilizing somehow, and we found out later, according to medical records, her oxygen level had dropped to 30 percent that afternoon, which isn't compatible with human life. She was in ICU in critical condition for two days, yet we believe Father Solanus interceded for her once again, and her current return to health is a testimony to the miraculous intercession of Blessed Father Solanus Casey, so we now "Thank God ahead of time" for her continued wonderful healthy life! Jan is now in her seventies.

"Blessed be God in all his designs!" ❖

The tooth of the matter

Father Tom Nguyen, O.F.M. Cap., as told to Linda Leist

The following is a commonly told story at the Solanus Casey Center in Detroit, Michigan.

On a warm summer day, a fellow friar in the novitiate came to see Father Solanus, in need of a healing miracle. He had a bad toothache, and if things went poorly at the dentist's office, this friar could miss too much formation and be sent back to the beginning of his novitiate, as was the practice at the time.

The young friar sought Father Solanus' blessing before leaving to see the dentist. The kindly priest told him to trust God that everything would work out.

While the friar was at the dentist, a lady who came to visit brought Father Solanus two ice cream cones. Too busy to eat them at the moment, Father Solanus shoved the two ice cream cones into his desk drawer, much to the dismay of his secretary, who was sure they would be a soupy mess in a matter of minutes.

More than a half-hour later, the young friar returned from the dentist, his tooth found to be miraculously healthy. He went to thank Father Solanus, who then pulled out three (not two!) perfectly frozen ice cream cones from his desk drawer on that hot summer day, which he offered to the friar to help celebrate his happy, healthy outcome! ❖

His work continues

By Joan Lasek

Joan Lasek

A few years ago, a friend from Huntington, Jan Scher, invited me to visit. I have known Jan since 2001 and have been blessed by taking several pilgrimage trips with her, including a trip to Ireland. She wanted to show me St. Felix Friary, where Blessed Solanus Casey had served the Catholic population of Huntington, Indiana from 1946 to 1956.

The friary was then in renovation mode. We approached the building that hot summer day, and I noticed several motorcycles parked on the terrace where the entrance to the building was located. My thoughts were that maybe the building was being vandalized by a bunch of rebel bikers.

Being late in the afternoon we paused, and a flurry of men came out of the building and mounted the motorcycles. Later we were informed that they were the craftsmen who were working on the interior projects.

We toured the lower level, making our way to the upper hallways where the cells of the monks lined the walls. Jan pointed out the cell where Father Solanus had slept and prayed, a small twin-sized bed and a small wooden piece of furniture that could have been used as a desk.

On the wall outside of his cell was a framed history and picture of Father Solanus, so we stopped to view it. My eyes were drawn toward the center of the hallway when I saw a monk dressed in a dark brown habit of a Franciscan monk with a long white beard cross the hallway from one of the cells to the opposite wall, entering the door of a cell. He moved slowly with his head down toward the doorway.

I turned to Jan and asked her if she had seen the monk. I assumed that there may be visitors in the building, and was surprised when she replied no, she had not seen the monk. Was my imagination getting the best of me? We continued on to the other end of the hallway and stopped in the living quarters of the caretakers of the monastery, who were supervising the project under construction.

Later I met Rob Mayo, who had arrived at the friary, and he chatted with Jan for a few minutes. I asked him if he had seen anything unusual in the building. He said his wife had, and recently one of the men working on the lower level had mentioned something. He did not elaborate on what he had seen. I thank the Lord and I am confident that Father Solanus is continuing his work at the St. Felix Center where he lived and prayed and worshipped his God so many years ago. ❖

'I love you, mom'

Audrey Peterson (Harber) as told to Linda Leist

A retreat at St. Felix Friary, in Huntington, afforded Audrey Harber the opportunity to learn about Father Solanus Casey, who once lived there. His gentle, powerful intercession became manifest to her when shortly after the retreat a young lady, age 27, McKenzie, was involved in a devastating automobile accident.

McKenzie was employed by Audrey's husband so she and her husband, in addition to family and friends, began their prayer campaign.

McKenzie had suffered a severed brainstem, was comatose, and put on a ventilator. She was deemed brain dead with no brain activity on the MRI. Doctors gave her no hope of recovering, and after two weeks her discharge orders were written so she could go home to die.

However, despite the dismal news, Audrey continued to pray for Father Solanus to intercede for McKenzie and restore her health despite a severed brain stem. That same night, after discharge orders were given, McKenzie was taken off the ventilator and her oxygen level dropped to fifty percent. Audrey continued to pray, and that night McKenzie surprised everyone by sitting up, now wide awake, and said, "I love you, mom."

No one can explain the medical miracle, and to everyone's amazement, within two weeks she was talking and eating, with the current MRI still showing no brain activity!

McKenzie continued to recover in unexpected ways, and Audrey said that if a miracle is supposed to happen, it will, when we keep the faith and keep praying, as Father Solanus taught, and continues to teach us! ❖

V   A silent partner

Gaby Mayo as told to Linda Leist

Gaby Mayo

Gaby Mayo, a very special spiritual friend of Father Solanus Casey, fills the roles of retreat coordinator, housekeeper, groundskeeper, and caretaker of St. Felix Catholic Center, where Father Solanus once lived.

She related a middle-of-the-night-event in which she believes Father Solanus was present and listening in her time of need. She had been waiting until 3 a.m. for a retreat group coming from Miami, Florida.

After their arrival she checked everyone in and was ready to go home. She quickly started walking down the steep concrete steps, and hurrying through the darkness she missed the last two steps.

In a flash of pain, she heard the cracking sound of a bone breaking. She had landed on the outer edge of her right food and immediately knew she had a serious break.

She crawled back to the stairs and sat there, praying, and begging Father Solanus to intercede for her. Tearfully, she made her way to his statue and continued to pray. She begged for the honor of continuing to serve him, which she knew she couldn't do with a broken foot or ankle.

She then hopped to her car on one foot and was able to drive herself home using only her left foot.

Her husband took her to RediMed later that morning, where tests revealed no broken bones, even though she had seen her foot flop sideways at the time of the fall!

To this day, Gaby states that she knows Father Solanus answered her prayers and keeps her close in her daily care of St. Felix. She senses his presence and is grateful for his inspirations. God is good! ❖

An electrifying experience with Father Solanus

Patrick Kelker as told to Linda Leist

Patrick Kelker

I was born in September 1953 at St. Joseph Hospital, Fort Wayne, Indiana.

Early in my life my mother told me that a special monk blessed all the babies individually, including me. She said she couldn't remember who the monk was. I would like to think that this special blessing came from Father Solanus Casey, even though it hasn't been verified.

In 1993 at the age of 40, I decided to live my faith instead of just going through the motions. My life up to that point was going to Mass on Sunday and pulling God down off the shelf when I needed something. After this I would go about my life rarely putting God into it. It certainly wasn't living what one would call an apostolic lifestyle.

Once I made this decision it wasn't long before I heard about Father Solanus Casey. I was really interested about learning of him, and shortly thereafter a kind woman gave me a bag full of information about him. It was from this information I learned he was in the process of becoming a saint. I remembered from my Catholic upbringing about the intercession of the saints and especially how God works miracles through a holy individual who is being considered for sainthood.

I wasn't petitioning God for a miracle, but I was asking for a special blessing through the intercession of Father Solanus Casey. It wasn't an elaborate prayer, it was just a simple, "Father Solanus, please ask God to give me a special blessing." I would say this prayer every evening as I prepared for sleep.

This went on for several months and one evening my wife awoke me and told me that there was a man standing by the entrance of our bedroom.

I was very tired that evening and I told her I was not very happy about being awakened. A few minutes later she once again said the man was still there.

I was very nearsighted and when I looked, I saw nothing, and I pleaded with her to go to sleep. Later for a third time she advised me that the man was still there, but he didn't look threatening. Suddenly, a light bulb went on in my head. I remembered my simple prayer to God. I said softly, "Father Solanus, if you are here for this blessing I've been praying for, here I am."

Immediately an electrical current started from the tip of my head and continued through my whole body to the bottom of my feet. My wife and I both fell asleep after this. We both found this hard to believe the next morning when we awoke and discussed what had taken place.

Shortly after receiving this blessing, I was on fire with the Holy Spirit. I wasn't sure about Father Solanus actually being in our room that evening, but I was living proof that something astonishing had happened.

It was shortly thereafter while visiting the 24-hour eucharistic adoration chapel, a lady that was just leaving as I was arriving handed me a copy of Catherine Odell's book about Solanus Casey.

I brought it home to read and my wife noticed it and exclaimed, "That's the man who was at the entrance to our bedroom the night you received that blessing!" I was glad to have this confirmation.

In late 1994 I made a pilgrimage, which included a visit for most of a day at a monastery. While making this visit, I became aware that everywhere I went on the grounds a monk was right behind me. After about two hours this monk came from behind to in front of me and said, "I've been asked to give you a special blessing from God. Will you accept it?"

My mind raced back to that simple prayer I made not long ago for Father Solanus' intercession, and I said, "Of course."

The monk placed his hand on my heart and prayed and once again the electrical current went from my head to my toes. The monk was not Father Solanus, but I'm sure that he directed him to me.

After receiving this blessing, God directed me to Father Eugene Koers, who became my spiritual director.

Father Koers introduced me to the Blessed Virgin Mary and took me to the Marian shrines in France and Spain. Father Koers showed me that devotion to God's mother was the surest path to heaven.

These past 25 years have been spent using all the graces I received from that special visit from Father Solanus Casey to share with others helping them to love God as I do.

I would like to think that blessing received as a newborn in 1953 did indeed come from the hand of Father Solanus.

Deo Gratias. ❖

Say a little prayer

Nancy Steinhofer as told to Linda Leist

My dad shared this with me many years ago. His name was Dr. John William Hohe, a dentist in Huntington, Indiana. This was at the start of his practice, sometime between 1946 and 1951, in Huntington. Father Solanus had come in to see my dad to have a tooth pulled.

Dad was unable to stop the bleeding on the tooth. My dad became very nervous and was pacing around. Father Solanus asked what was wrong and dad said that he was unable to get the bleeding stopped. Father asked for a quiet room where he could pray, so he was led to where we developed our x-rays. Fifteen minutes later he emerged from the room and the bleeding had stopped. ❖

Father Solanus' powerful intercession

Suzanne Federspiel as told to Linda Leist

Suzanne Federspiel, age thirty, was involved in a head-on collision, each driver estimated to be driving sixty miles per hour, and her car had to be cut apart to get her out. Nearly every bone in her body was broken and her leg was said to be crushed beyond repair. The attending doctor could not detect a pulse in it, so in order to avoid the possibility of gangrene he prescribed amputation below the knee to be done the next morning.

Her father, familiar with the powerful intercession of Father Solanus Casey, asked the doctor to please wait one more day, as the family wanted to pray. The doctor agreed but stated firmly no more than one day.

The family prayed to Father Solanus, asking him to intercede for Suzanne, and the very next day the doctor felt a pulse and knew that there was life in the leg and did not amputate below the knee. He did remove one-half inch of her baby toe, but Suzanne and her family are deeply grateful for the intercession of Father Solanus, believing he interceded for the miracle, and now she even has a leg to stand on!

Later in life, when Suzanne and her husband wanted to start a family, she discovered she was unable to have babies.

Father Solanus continued to intercede, perhaps, because it so happened that a coworker with several children didn't see how she could adequately care for the baby she was soon to deliver.

However, arrangements were made so that Suzanne and her husband found themselves the proud parents of a one-day-old baby boy, once again the answer to their prayers!

An extra blessing for the happy new family was that even though policy at Suzanne's workplace only allowed a three-week maternity leave, her coworkers split up her hours so that she could spend months, instead of weeks, home with her beautiful new baby. ❖

Two grace-filled phone calls

Theresa M. Gabet as told to Linda Leist

Theresa M. Gabet

In 1955, my sister, Lioba R., began hemorrhaging while pregnant with Stanley, her eighth child. I called Father Solanus Casey since he was in Huntington, Indiana, at the time, and told him the situation. I told Father Solanus that Lioba had a large family and that we were all very concerned about her.

Father Solanus said to me on the phone, "I think the Good Lord will smile upon her."

Shortly after I hung up the phone, we received a call saying that Stan was born, and my sister and her baby were doing well.

Another time I called Father Solanus in the early 1950s, but I don't remember the exact year.

My good friend, Betty N., was in the hospital for surgery to remove a kidney tumor. I called Father Solanus to ask him to pray for her and he told me, "I think she will be pleasantly surprised."

They did an x-ray before taking her to surgery and the tumor was gone.

Later on, we found out from Betty's daughter that Betty had actually gone to Huntington to talk to Father Solanus about the tumor and surgery. Father Solanus told Betty, "Don't worry, you won't have the surgery." ❖

Rosaries made from nature

Lynn (Scheiber) Belding as told to Danny Bickel

There were a few trees in the front yard of St. Felix Friary. The trees were filled with pods and inside the pods were small seeds, or beads.

Father Solanus had an idea to make rosaries out of the beads. Lynn recalled visiting Father Solanus, as she and her mother, Mary Scheiber, did many times. Father Solanus asked Lynn to gather the pods that had fallen to the ground. As she collected them, Father Solanus held open the pockets of his robe and Lynn filled both sides.

He then gave the beads to the brothers, who boiled them in a large kettle. They next dried the beads, which made them very hard.

Francis Shaw, who owned a machine shop, was given the beads to drill a hole through each bead for the next step in making the rosaries. Lynn said "Uncle Francy" had a lot of time invested in the beads, but he was happy to help Father Solanus.

The beads were then given to Mary. She was a widow, and one of the ways she made money was by making rosaries. Lynn didn't recall who bought the rosaries or if any survived, but if any did, the persons in possession of one of them has a secondhand relic from the hands of Father Solanus Casey.

Mary took a picture of Father Solanus, with a crucifix superimposed. It was taken about 70 years ago (1954). Mary took it with her little Brownie camera, with which she would double expose photos. It is not a coincidence this picture turned out so well. ❖

A favor granted to a Capuchin's mother

By Brother John Francis Samsa, O.F.M. Cap.

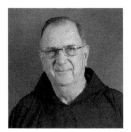

Brother John Francis Samsa, O.F.M. Cap.

My greatest joy of studying at St. Felix Friary in Huntington, Indiana, was the opportunity of living with Father Solanus Casey from 1955 through 1956. Father Solanus has now since been declared "Blessed" Solanus Casey on Nov. 18, 2017.

I remember one evening, around 7 p.m., when I received a call from my brother Donald telling me that our mother had a very serious health condition. The doctors had failed to dissolve a blood clot in her left arm and it was now passing through her body. I was told that if it went to her lungs or to her heart it could be fatal.

I immediately went up to Father Solanus' room to ask him to pray for my mother. As was the custom, I gave the usual greeting and knelt in his doorway and explained to him my mother's serious health condition and asked if he would please pray for her.

Father Solanus had two ways of answering your request. In his very soft, high-pitched voice, he would either say, "Ohhh, God's will be done," or he would say, "Ohhhh, I will pray for her."

If his response was the first one, it would mean that you had better prepare yourself for the worst and accept God's will for whatever sad or difficult news might come your way in the near future. But if his response was the latter, that meant you need not worry and you should "thank God ahead of time" (a favorite saying of Solanus) because everything was going to work out just fine.

You can imagine my feeling of relief when Father Solanus said, "Ohhh, I will pray for her," and not only that but I can still picture him as he scooted past me and literally flew down the corridor, with his sandals flapping, to the chapel to pray for my mother.

I can't tell you how relieved I was. I went to bed that night and slept well without a worry on my mind about my mother. That is the trust and confidence that we all had in Father Solanus' prayers when he promised to pray for whatever you requested of him.

A couple of days later I received a call from my brother Donald telling me that our mother was out of danger. The blood clot had passed through her body and came out in her right arm and the doctors were able to dissolve it without any further complications and my mother was free of all danger. My brother was somewhat taken back by my casual calm remark when I said: "Oh, I knew mom would be all right because Father Solanus went down to the chapel immediately that night to pray for her."

Take it for what it is worth. It could have been just the nature of such things, but for me it was a "miracle" worked by our merciful God through the intercession of Blessed Father Solanus Casey. My mother went on to live a very healthy life for 45 more years and died a peaceful, natural death at the age of 96. ❖

• • •

Please, do not disturb

There is another incident worth mentioning that many of us friars who were in formation at the time at St. Felix Friary in Huntington, Indiana, can still recall. One evening, when the entire teaching staff was at a faculty meeting, Father Solanus, who was not a member of the faculty, led us in evening prayer.

Since it was a Friday, we were praying the Stations of the Cross. When Father Solanus got to the Third Station he went into ecstasy and just remained there on his knees, wrapped in silent contemplative prayer. We waited for several minutes for him to continue the Way of the Cross, but nothing happened, and he just remained there motionless, wrapped in prayer, on his knees.

When we young friars eventually became restless, the senior friar, Father Timon Costello, told us all to go to our rooms to study because it looked like we would be here all night waiting for Father Solanus to continue leading us in the Way of the Cross. All 60 of us left the chapel without Father Solanus being disturbed from his ecstasy and mystical prayer.

Sure enough, the following morning Father Solanus was found sleeping on the floor in front of the Blessed Sacrament altar. ❖

Miracles do happen

By Carolyn Butler

Anthony Butler (second from left) as an altar server.

At six months of age my brother, Tony, was found to have a hole in the upper chamber of his heart. The doctors called it a heart murmur. When Tony's grandmother's mother, Mrs. Ucker, found out, she gave him a relic badge of Father Solanus Casey. My mom pinned it to his clothing every day.

Mrs. Ucker was also helped by Father Solanus. She and her daughter visited him, and he blessed and prayed for her heart problem. The next time she went to the doctor, her heart problem was gone. She promotes Father Solanus today, and thanks God for the many miracles he lets happen.

Tony went through many X-rays and EKGs. In August 1992, his hole was still there, yet he didn't show any signs of being ill. He was very strong and active, which were all good signs. On Jan. 29, 1993, the doctors said his hole was gone. We were very blessed for a healthy and happy little boy. We thank God and Father Solanus every day.

Our family joined the Father Solanus Guild, and we reported our miracle. We are praying that someday Father Solanus will become a saint.

Father Solanus was a grade-school dropout and a failure in the seminary. He failed at everything except what counted. Born to Irish-Catholic parents in a log cabin in Wisconsin, he was baptized Bernard and became known as "Barney" to his family and friends. He loved baseball, hot dogs, had a sense of humor, a fine-tuned Irish wit, and could play a fair game of pool.

Later in his life, he became the tireless, brown-robed figure whom many people regarded as a saint. The list of special favors and healings, granted through his prayers and blessings, is long and varied. Among the many thousands whom Father Solanus has helped spiritually, physically, and emotionally, was a thirty-nine-year-old man from Michigan. He came to Father Solanus with stomach cancer, in great pain, and in very low spirits. He was afraid no one would be able to care for his children. Eight days after speaking with Father Solanus, he returned to him and said he was in no pain and totally recovered.

Another person was a thirty-year-old woman named Anna. She was taken from her Detroit home to the hospital for surgery. Doctors told her she had a brutal liver condition. Her sister phoned Father Solanus and he promised to pray for Anna. Less than a month later, Anna's sister told Father Solanus that Anna was already home and recovering. ❖

Juanita Castator – Prayers from Father Solanus

By Susan Castator Bentz Braden

Juanita Castator

My mom was born on Dec. 5, 1912. She was raised Methodist but converted to Catholicism as a young adult. She and my dad, Thais "Jack" Castator, were married in March 1941, and I was born in January 1942. We lived in Fort Wayne, Indiana.

Mom started to get sick around 1952-1953. The doctors in Fort Wayne could not find out what was wrong even after many tests. She was finally sent to Dr. Capps at St. Luke's Hospital in Chicago where she underwent more tests and procedures. During this time, they were giving her various treatments to alleviate the symptoms.

She was finally diagnosed with lymphatic leukemia and acute aplastic anemia; there were few if any treatments for this disease in the early 1950s. One symptom of her disease was an enlarged spleen, which grew to be the size of a watermelon. The doctors decided the spleen had to be removed as they feared she would not be able to live much longer since it was continuing to grow.

She was aware that she may not survive the surgery, and even purchased a dress in which to be buried. It was in the time before her surgery that she was told about a Father Solanus who was at St. Felix friary in Huntington, Indiana. She, along with her nephew Dick Lash, went to visit Father Solanus. Dick was a medical intern at St. Luke's. He had contracted hepatitis while treating a patient and was seriously ill.

On April 4, 1954, mom, Dick, and I made the trip to Huntington. I was twelve years old at the time but can still remember seeing Father Solanus in the office where he received visitors, and I remember how nice he was while talking to us. My mother told Father Solanus that her only wish was that she would live long enough to see me raised.

Juanita Castator's Seraphic Mass Association enrollment card she received from Blessed Solanus Casey.

He told her not to worry, that she would see me raised. He also spoke with my cousin Dick. He prayed with and blessed the three of us. He also gave mom a Seraphic Mass Association enrollment card, which he dated and signed as Fr. Bernard, OFM Cap., and wrote at the bottom "Blessed be God! In all His designs!" We still have this beautiful card.

Mom would faithfully pray the rosary every day and had a great devotion to Mary; she asked others to pray it for her while she would be unable to during her upcoming surgery. The doctors had a large supply of blood ready for transfusions due to the high risk of blood loss during the operation.

When they went in and removed the spleen, almost instantly her numbers and vitals turned around for the positive. The blood supply wasn't needed. At some point during or after the surgery, mom had a vision of the Virgin Mary standing over her, telling her not to worry, that everything would be OK. She saw Mary open a door and bright light flooded in around her. She said the vision was so clear, beautiful, and colorful.

The doctors were amazed at her recovery. She had no problems at all after the surgery and her tests came back clear. She had a miraculous healing by God through Father Solanus and the Blessed Mother! The doctors all told her that they did nothing to cure her of the disease, and it wasn't anything they did that caused her to live.

She would go back to Chicago periodically for tests, but never had any trace of the disease after that. Mom continued to say her daily rosary the rest of her life. She also continued to pray for Father Solanus' intercession in her life and made a trip at some point to Detroit to visit the St. Bonaventure Monastery where he had lived.

Mom lived a full and healthy life after her illness until 1989 when she had exploratory surgery for back pain. The doctors found that she had pancreatic cancer. She never woke up after that surgery and passed away on June 30, 1989, at the age of 76. Not only did she live to see me grow up, but she saw her three grandchildren grow up, too.

Her nephew, Dick, who visited Father Solanus with her, was also cured of his hepatitis. He went on to have a career as a doctor and also lived a full and healthy life after his illness. My daughter and I were able to attend the 2017 beatification Mass for Father Solanus in Detroit. We also visited St. Felix Friary (now St. Felix Catholic Center) in Huntington for the 2021 feast day celebration for Blessed Solanus Casey.

The woman who manages the building showed us the office where Father Solanus received visitors. It looks very similar to what I remember from 1954. ❖

A badges' blessing

By Marypat Hughes

Mrs. Burpoe gave me a Blessed Father Solanus Casey badge during the COVID-19 pandemic. I was a dietitian working in a nursing home. I lost my job and was devastated as I am a single mom.

I was unaware that I had a genetic disorder, which was diagnosed a couple of months later.

Due to this disorder, COVID-19 increases the rate of heart attacks. I feel Mrs. Burpoe may have helped save my life with her evangelization of Blessed Solanus. ❖

Too good to forget

By John Woods

John Woods, former editor-in-chief of Catholic New York, from which the following four reflections first appeared.

A couple of months ago, Catholic New York published a two-part series on the canonization causes of those who have a connection to New York. Those well-written articles, by Catholic New York's features editor Claudia McDonnell, looked at the lives of nine holy men and women who served the Church here in the Archdiocese of New York.

A couple of weeks ago a phone call came in from Edward Hawkins alerting us to a cause that we had missed. It was that of Father Solanus Casey, O.F.M. Cap., who had served for 20 years at three parishes in the archdiocese in the early part of his priesthood.

Hawkins ought to know about Father Solanus. He is president of the local chapter of the Father Solanus Guild known as Queen of All Saints Circle, St. John the Baptist, based at the Capuchin Franciscan-run St. John the Baptist Church on West 31st Street in Manhattan.

The 60-year-old Brooklyn resident has been involved with the guild for about three years after learning about Father Solanus from an EWTN program in which Father Benedict Groeschel, C.F.R., interviewed two Capuchin Franciscans involved in promoting their fellow friar's cause for canonization from the guild's headquarters in Detroit.

Hawkins then read a notice in Catholic New York's "Out and About" section about the Queen of All Saints Circle, and soon became involved with its activities. He served as secretary of the circle before his election as president.

Interestingly, Hawkins said, "the lack of the spectacular" in Father

Solanus' life story made a positive impression on him. In his first priestly assignment at Sacred Heart Church in Yonkers, where he would serve for 14 years, Father Solanus was sacristan and doorkeeper and directed the Young Ladies Sodality and the altar boys. A guild brochure about the friar's life highlights his prayerful example at Mass and his charity toward the sick, the children, non-Catholics, and the poor.

"He had a very simple, gentle way of dealing with people and counseling them. ... It made me realize that he was a holy and dedicated person," Hawkins told me over the phone.

Father Solanus would later serve at the Capuchin-run parishes of Our Lady of Sorrows in lower Manhattan and the former Our Lady of Angels in East Harlem, as well as St. Michael's in the East New York section of Brooklyn.

He also served for many years at St. Bonaventure Friary in Detroit, where he became well known for his ministry of charity and comfort, especially during the Great Depression, when his concern for the poor led the Capuchins there to open a soup kitchen.

Some two decades after Father Solanus' death in 1957, Cardinal John Deardon, then archbishop of Detroit, initiated the cause. It received official approval from Pope John Paul II in 1982. Thirteen years later, the pope promulgated a decree citing the "heroic virtues" of Father Solanus and declared him "Venerable."

Hawkins said the goal of the Queen of All Saints Circle is to keep alive the memory of Father Solanus by spreading word of his works and promoting his cause. There are currently about 90 active members, with about one-third attending the monthly meetings at St. John the Baptist on the second Saturday, beginning at 10 a.m. Along with regular business, members recite the rosary and attend Mass in the church. Father Philip Fabiano, O.F.M. Cap., pastor of St. John the Baptist, is the circle's spiritual moderator.

As he looks forward, Hawkins said he hopes the circle's members will be able to introduce word of Father Solanus to schools and nursing homes in the area through speaking engagements and by sending out printed materials and videos.

The legacy of Father Solanus is never far from what they do. As he greeted people with kindness and compassion, he did it in the name of the Church he served so well, Hawkins said. "There was always a spiritual component to his work," he said. "That's something we need to do now more than ever." ❖

— Published in the Dec. 31, 2009, issue of Catholic New York

• • •

Father Solanus at the DMV

I'm no different from most New Yorkers when it comes to visiting the State Department of Motor Vehicles. The quicker I can move from station to station and complete my business, the happier I am.

On the morning of New Year's Eve, I noticed that my license renewal, due shortly, required an eye examination. It was a busy time in our household, with out-of-state relatives staying with us as we prepared for a family party the next day. So, my wife wasn't too pleased when I told her I was going to make a trip to the DMV.

I promised not to be too long and was happy to find out from a fellow customer in the parking lot that the line inside was moving. It took me about 10 minutes to get to the counter and just another minute to get my photo taken. Then it was off to the benches to wait for the eye exam.

After another 15 minutes, my number was called, and I advanced to the appointed window. At that point, the employee at that station stepped away for a moment. With little to do until she returned, I glanced down and couldn't believe what caught my eye. Under a clear mat at her workplace was a sheet of paper with the words "Solanus Casey" neatly hand-printed near the top. Also visible was a picture of Venerable Solanus Casey, the Capuchin Franciscan friar whose cause for canonization I had written about in this column. Ironically the column was written in our last issue, Dec. 31, the same day I happened to be at the DMV.

There was also some typed text on the page before me, including a quote from Father Solanus that read, "Man's greatness lies in being faithful to the present moment." Those words almost leapt off the page. They also must have inspired me because when the employee returned, I asked her if the information about Father Solanus belonged to her. She replied kindly that she had learned about him from a television program and that she had just recently put the clipping where it could be seen. Several people had glanced at in in recent days and she figured at least a few had looked him up on Google afterward.

During the course of our conversation, she mentioned that she admired Father Solanus for his gentle manner. She thought it had a lot to do with his willingness to really listen to everyone with whom he came in contact. She said that she also tried to be a good listener, at the DMV and to others she encountered.

I told her who I was and that I had written about Father Solanus. She asked me a couple questions about Catholic New York and my own feelings about Father Solanus.

For the rest of that day, and for the days that followed, I told the story of my special encounter at the DMV to many of those I met. It could be chalked up to a happy coincidence. But with all the obstacles and odds stacked against me ending up at precisely that window, I prefer to view the meeting another way.

For me, it was a moment of grace. When God puts you in a position to share an experience, he'll give you the words and the courage to step forward. You just have to do it. The whole exchange at the DMV didn't last more than a minute or two, but it had a great effect on me. It made me want to share the news of my own encounter with Father Solanus, and to learn more about him.

I passed the eye test, too. ❖

— Published in the Jan. 14, 2010, issue of Catholic New York

• • •

Surprised by Solanus

I am a Catholic through and through, right from the beginning, all the way through 16 years of elementary, high school, and college; 27 years (and counting) of marriage and family life; and a professional life largely spent working in the Catholic Press in New York. The religion runs deep with me, in ways in which I am not always even consciously aware.

The Church is a place where I find comfort, a sense of belonging, a valid and sustaining belief structure and a personal experience of God through the Mass, the sacraments, and the other people who share a worshiping community that dates to Jesus' time among us.

There is, however, one element of our Catholic faith that has always seemed to elude my understanding — sainthood. I should clarify that the elusiveness does not involve any teaching about the canonization process or the great mystical nature of some saints' lives and ministries.

It is a little more elemental than that. Many Catholic friends and colleagues have their favorite saints, whom they often follow with devotion and love. Two canonized saints, St. Pope John Paul II and St. Teresa of Calcutta, both have legions of devotees, as do St. Frances Xavier Cabrini and St. Elizabeth Ann Seton, who are both known for their works of service and holiness in New York.

While I admire all of those saints, I don't have a deep personal connection with any of them. There is one future (hopefully) saint with whom I do feel a bond. We wrote about Capuchin Franciscan Father Solanus Casey in our last issue when Pope Francis announced that his cause for beatification has been approved and that Father Solanus will be beatified later this year in Detroit, where he spent most of his long priestly ministry.

My interest in Father Solanus stems from back-to-back columns I wrote in late 2009 and early 2010. The first one was sparked when he was inadvertently left out of a series we published about New Yorkers whose causes for canonization were open. After all, Father Solanus served here in the archdiocese for 20 years near the beginning of the 20th century, the bulk of that time at Capuchin-run Sacred Heart Church in Yonkers as well as shorter tenures at Our Lady of Sorrows in Lower Manhattan and the former Our Lady Queen of Angels in East Harlem. He also served at St. Michael's Church in the Diocese of Brooklyn.

So, Father Solanus was a New Yorker. That's the first reason I like him. If that were the only connection, I never would have written the second column. That one was sparked when I went to the Department of Motor Vehicles to renew my driver's license.

As I advanced to the window for my eye exam, I glanced down at the clerk's workspace and saw a sheet of paper with a picture of Father Solanus, with his name neatly hand-printed, and a typed quote of his before me. It read, "Man's greatness lies in being faithful to the present moment."

I could not resist asking the clerk about her Father Solanus trove. She explained that she had recently seen a television program about him and that she admired his gentle manner. She thought it had a lot to do with his willingness to listen to others, and she said she tried to follow his example in that regard.

At that time, I squirreled away some Father Solanus materials of my own, holy cards sent by a few readers along with booklets about the Capuchin Franciscan priest. In subsequent years, I'd add a bit more from time to time. I looked around for them this past week when I knew I was writing this column and found them tucked away in a drawer in my bedside nightstand.

Father Solanus often shows up in unlikely places where I least expect to encounter him. Capuchin Franciscan priests and others who know much more than I do about his life say that my experience is not unique. I look forward to more surprises in the future. ❖

— Published in the May 25, 2017, issue of Catholic New York

• • •

This valedictorian's story is worth a close read

I won't soon forget my first experience with John Evans, and I sincerely doubt that it will be the last time I hear his name. In fact, we all may be hearing from the young man quite a bit in the future.

For the uninitiated, Evans received the Carty Valedictory Medal and spoke on behalf of the class of 2017 at Manhattan College's undergraduate commencement May 19.

The English major, with a double minor in history and medieval studies, compiled a 3.94 GPA at Manhattan. He also has published numerous literary works, including two poetry collections, and has been known to perform at open mic nights with his folk-rock band.

You should also know that he is visually impaired, having lost his sight except for an ability to distinguish light and shadow and, occasionally, the outlines of objects.

I wanted to note his accomplishments before his blindness, not because it isn't significant but because John has a lot more to his story than his disability.

He was only five when he lost his sight. For more than a decade, he believed the cause was a rare genetic disorder, which was his official diagnosis. About two-and-a-half-years ago, he learned that his blindness was caused by a brain tumor that pressed upon his optic nerves.

You might imagine that his new diagnosis raised questions of his mortality, his place in the world, and the immortality of his soul. Those aren't my words. They were the way this very devout Catholic expressed his response during our phone conversation.

He can cover a lot of theological ground in a short period of time, telling how he steeped himself in the Old and New Testament and read St. Teresa of Ávila's spiritual masterpiece, "Interior Castle," while preparing for his surgery.

He said he spent a number of post-surgery hours in total darkness before light finally began "seeping in."

"My first thought was, will I ever see something as simple as light again?"

He knew that his goal of becoming a professor of medieval literature would be possible only if he could resume his classes amid the trials of his medical exams and testing as he endured the recovery period after surgery.

As Evans explained in his valedictory address, he was not able to accomplish the great things he did by himself. At the crux of his speech, he said, was a theological lesson based on the definition of the Greek word for church, or "ecclesia."

"We are all called out to help one another, as people helped me for the past four years," he said. "From the students who held a door for me, to students who guided me to class, they proved they were called out to greatness."

The same could be said for Evans, who does not plan to slow down any time soon. He will pursue his master's degree and doctorate in medieval studies at Fordham University.

Evans' family, including his parents Robert and Eileen, and his brother, Brian, who just completed his freshman year at Manhattan, have played a major role in his victories.

His full name is John Casey Solanus Evans, and one of the first things he told me when we spoke was of his grandparents' devotion to the Capuchin friar who will be beatified later this year. His family's parish is Sacred Heart in Yonkers, where Father Solanus served for 14 years in the first part of the 20th century.

He and his family pray regularly at the friar's shrine in their parish church, and he said that he hopes one day to be healed of his blindness through the intercession of Father Solanus.

Evans has a wisdom that is well beyond his years, and a personal faith that is inspiring on many levels. At the close of our conversation, he said his thoughts and prayers were with me that morning and that he would be grateful, no matter if I wrote a sentence, or five, about our exchange.

"My way of reaching other people has been through my story," he said. "If God is the primary storyteller, he tells his story through our lives." ❖

— Published in the June 8, 2017, issue of Catholic New York

An instant healing

Donna Shaw as told to Linda Leist

Donna Shaw, 88, recalled a meeting with Father Solanus from her childhood.

She was about five years old when she noticed increasing pain on the lower right side of her abdomen. She was diagnosed with appendicitis, and her parents, Paul and Evelyn Krumanaker, faith-filled people, put their trust in the Lord and were inspired to quickly take her to St. Felix Friary, the residence of Father Solanus Casey. Many people in the Huntington, Indiana area and elsewhere had reported favors granted through the intercession of this holy, gifted priest.

He gently spoke with Donna and her parents to determine the child's needs. He then reverently prayed for Donna's healing, interceding with Our Lord on her behalf.

Soon she noticed that the pain she was suffering from was gone, never to recur. She and her parents were greatly relieved when they saw that she was healed, and they thanked Our Lord for the healing through Father Solanus' intercession. ❖

'Will I ever walk again?'

By Irene Milko Cooper, courtesy of Janine Ayres, Irene's daughter

I was nine years old in the summer of 1934. I don't think I will ever forget that year. It was July, a nice balmy day and my father and his friend Mike were going to Belle Isle to fish. My brother Gene and I went with them to play along the Detroit River waterfront. I loved Belle Isle! It will always be special to me. It was our only introduction to country living.

We lived in the heart of the factory industry surrounded by Midland Steel, Packard motor car company, Chrysler, Ford, and General Motors. We took off with a nice lunch, but my left knee was sore as I had fallen three times on the same knee on the school cement playground and it had not healed so it was an open sore; no bandage could stay on it and Band-Aids had not yet been invented.

I remember getting sand on it as we made sandcastles and figures in the sand. Years later I thought maybe the polio germs got in this way. That night I remember I started to limp and the next day it seemed I could not straighten up my leg. The following night I had a horrible nightmare!

I was on a spinning top, and I would spin round and round and out and then back again. Also, I was so hot. Burning up. I must've screamed because I found my parents by my bed. As I focused them into sight, my mom placed a cold washcloth on my forehead and that helped. The next day I couldn't stand. My leg would not support me. My father took me to the children's hospital. They took children whose parents couldn't pay.

I remember crying softly all the way there. I was so scared. My dad carried me in and they put a gown on me with a slit in the back. I was terribly embarrassed in front of these strange people! A few moments later a nice, gentle doctor came in. I found out that these incredible doctors volunteered their time and services for free. The doctor I had was from France. He spoke broken English so he hardly spoke to me, but his smile, kindness, and concern was felt by me and I immediately felt better about being in the hospital.

Later I would discover that he used an experimental therapy that might have saved me from becoming permanently crippled. He used the "Sister Kenny" method to treat polio (a reference to Elizabeth Kenny as a senior nurse, not a religious sister). My leg was stretched by weights as by now it was bent all the time. I was then put in a medicated body cast along with my complete left leg. I was in the hospital for one week. The nurses were good to me, and I loved the food.

I was in a cast for six months during the hottest part of Michigan's humid summers. It was unbearably itchy and uncomfortable and so very hot. Our house had no insulation. We never owned a fan. I could not sit in a cool bathtub of water. How I longed for that luxury! After three months I had to have the cast removed and the leg checked. Nowadays I think they use a saw of some kind but at the time they used shears like big scissors that cut right off the sides of the cast from under my armpit to my ankle.

Many times they cut the skin and I'd cry out in pain. The person cutting would try not to but it was impossible because the skin was folded, loose, and sagging. How sad I was when I was told I had to have another cast put on to ensure the progress I was making. All I could think about was that heavy cast would have to be cut off again.

At home I was told to lie flat on my back in bed and stay there, but this was making me dizzy and weak, plus just going to the bathroom or trying to walk was murder. Eventually I cracked the cast at the groin and was able to walk around the house like Frankenstein! And before I knew it I was going all over the place and doing most things. I remember the day I was discharged as cured. That was what the hospital said.

My mother and I were dropped off at the hospital by a friend who had to leave. It was a cold, snowy day and it seemed like we waited forever. They cut my cast off and I cried as they cut my skin in several places again. My leg looked horrible. I tried not to look at it. It looked like a stick with hanging flesh on it, some of it peeling like a bad sunburn.

I could not bend the knee, but the doctor said that would come with time and exercise. I remember the day I was discharged. My mom had brought my long underwear stockings and shoes. It felt so funny to have them on with no feeling, really. They gave me crutches to use and I felt so clumsy and afraid. I thought if I fell, that stick of a leg of mine would crack and break.

We finally got outside. Snow had accumulated. Afraid of falling on the ice, we had no car, so we waited for a streetcar. My mother and I and the crutches somehow got onto the streetcar and then made it back off and I walked the two blocks through the alley behind our house. By this time I was exhausted, cold, had no gloves and my fingers were numb, and my legs were shaking. So mom, God bless her heart, carried me piggyback the rest of the way home. It was so good to be in the house. I just collapsed. My brothers gathered. Gene didn't say anything. Eddie looked shocked. He said, "Will your leg ever look like the other one again? It sure looks skinny."

Eventually, I could stand up and my leg supported me. First, I would lean against the wall. My mother, my dad, and anybody around would help steady me. My knee would not bend even though I tried to exercise it a little every day. It seemed locked in a straight position, and I remember also thinking, "Will I ever walk again?" I couldn't believe it, but I even missed the clumsy heavy cast for the support it gave me.

One day a neighbor came to visit us and told my mother about a priest at the Capuchin Monastery in Detroit who performed miracles. His name I will never forget. It was Father Solanus Casey. She suggested that my mom and dad take me to see him, so I was bundled up and placed in their car and delivered to Father Solanus.

After waiting in a very long line he motioned me to approach. My parents guided me to him, and I was placed on his lap. He prayed, looked at me and said, "Dear God, this little girl would like to run and play like her friends. Heal her legs so she can do this." He placed his hand on my knee and gave me a kind smile. I did not walk at once, but the next day I crossed the room myself, stiff-legged. Within a week I was walking normally and before long you couldn't hold me down. I shall always be grateful to Father Solanus Casey for the miraculous healing he gave me.

Years later I learned that there were many others who'd been healed by him. The Church received dozens of letters throughout the years in praise of him. I'm also grateful to the doctor who prescribed my alternative treatment. Some doctors operated on polio patients with conventional surgery, and there were quite a few victims in our neighborhood who ended up crippled for life.

My doctor wrapped a cloth around the infected area, treated it with medication to draw out poisons, then fit the cast over it. Having polio changed my whole outlook on life. It made me everlastingly thankful for the sheer pleasure of being able to walk, to work, to dance, and to run. It taught me patience.

At one time before I contracted polio the girls at school remarked that my legs were somewhat bowed, and I felt self-conscious about it. After the polio I could care less. I was just thankful that I could walk. It gave me time to stop and think of others and I used to think, "At least I have my eyesight and I can see the roses bloom and the sun, the stars, and the moon." I do believe that would be the hardest thing to cope with, blindness.

Many polio victims during that time never regained the ability to walk. They were crippled for life, but I believe that the experimental technique that the French doctor used with me, the "Sister Kenny" method and Father Solanus Casey's miraculous healing prayer gave me my life back. I will be forever grateful to them all and I often wish I could go back in time to thank them. ❖

Editor's note: Irene passed away at the age of 93.

Blessed Solanus Casey inducted into 2021 class of Huntington County Honors

Courtesy of the Huntington County TAB weekly newspaper

Blessed Solanus Casey, who lived at St. Felix Friary in Huntington, Indiana, from 1946 to 1956, was inducted into the 2021 class of Huntington County Honors on Oct. 21, 2021, in the rotunda of the Huntington County Courthouse.

He was inducted along with eleven other Huntington County honorees whose lifetime achievements and works were recognized.

Created in 2014, Huntington County Honors highlights both the famous and those who are less well known. Candidates must have made a lasting impact on Huntington County or brought recognition to the community through their actions or achievements in one of five categories: athletics and recreation, business and professional, community and public service, humanities and cultural, and historical.

Huntington County Honors inducted its first class in 2016. This year's class was originally selected in 2020, but the ceremony was canceled due to the COVID-19 pandemic, and the class was carried over to 2021.

"In addition to recognizing outstanding individuals, we have a goal to preserve legacies that might otherwise be lost to history," said Paul Siegfried, a member of the board of directors of Huntington County Honors. "Each year, in our research, we continue to uncover remarkable people and their stories, and we take great pride in presenting them to the Huntington [County] community."

Father Solanus Casey was a simple, humble man of God who spent much of his life among the poor and infirm. He was known for his inspirational words and healing hand that followed him through his mission life, including the ten years he spent in Huntington at St. Felix Friary late in his life. In 2017, Father Solanus was bestowed the title of "Blessed" in a beatification ceremony in Detroit, the final step before sainthood.

Information on all the inductees is available on the Huntington County Honors website at huntingtoncountyhonors.org., and a photo and bio of each inductee is on display at the Huntington County Historical Museum in Huntington. ❖

Prayer for the canonization of Blessed Solanus Casey

O God, I adore You. I give myself to You. May I be the person You want me to be, and May Your will be done in my life today.

I thank You for the gifts You gave Father Solanus. If it is Your Will, bless us with the Canonization of Father Solanus so that others may imitate and carry on his love for all the poor and suffering of our world.

As he joyfully accepted Your divine plans, I ask You, according to Your Will, to hear my prayer for ... (your intention) through Jesus Christ Our Lord. Amen.

"Blessed be God in all His Designs." ❖

'Thank God Ahead of Time'

By Danny Bickel

We have been honored here at Sts. Peter and Paul Church in Huntington, Indiana.

An anonymous person has graciously donated a robe, which is believed to have belonged to Blessed Father Solanus Casey. Our pastor, Father Tony Steinacker, has accepted the robe and had a great idea that enhanced Blessed Solanus' humbleness and spirituality.

Sts. Peter and Paul has constructed a building located behind the church. Presently, the building is used for meetings, parish gatherings, prayer groups, and other parish activities. Father Tony encased the robe in a large wooden frame with a glass front.

All parishioners and guests visiting our new building will have an opportunity to view the encased robe. Bishop Kevin Rhoades dedicated the building on April 24, 2024, in honor of Blessed Solanus. It is named The Blessed Father Solanus Casey Center.

Father Tony, with the permission of Bishop Rhoades, commissioned a portrait of Blessed Solanus, which adorns the sanctuary of our church, where our inspiration and devotion to him is evident.

Many Catholics in Huntington and others in parishes in New York, Brooklyn, Detroit, and elsewhere have had close and personal relationships with Blessed Solanus. We know he will eventually be canonized a saint in the Roman Catholic Church.

We are truly blessed to have a strong connection between our city, our two parishes, and other parishes, and so many of us personally, with Blessed Father Solanus Casey.

May we all thank God ahead of time. ❖

Never-ending story

This little book is about Blessed Father Solanus Casey, O.F.M. Cap., and the memories he left behind with those who knew him, knew about him, or who experienced favors granted through his intercession.

There are many more stories that should be told, even if they are published after his canonization, and there are still many alive today who have memories of him, as well as children and relatives of those who actually encountered his graces, who have not had those stories of their deceased loved ones shared for everyone of faith to enjoy and from which to be inspired to love God more deeply.

I humbly request that contributors send their stories and a printed photo of themselves as well. Mail your stories and photos to Richard G. Beemer, 997N-300W, Huntington, IN 46750, or email the stories only to richardbeemer8@gmail.com. All printed photos must be sent by mail. When I receive your submission, I will email or send by mail a permission form that needs to be completed and returned to me at the above postal address or email address. It is required by the publisher. Thank you and God bless you.

About the editors

Richard G. Beemer has worked and continues his vocation as an editor in the Catholic press. For 31 years he worked at Our Sunday Visitor as an associate editor and later as managing editor of Our Sunday Visitor's weekly national newspaper and other periodicals. He's also edited, yet mostly proofread, more than three-hundred books for Our Sunday Visitor, Catholic Answers, and numerous other Catholic publishing companies, which he continues to do. He is currently the managing editor, copy editor, and proofreader for Angelus magazine, the official biweekly publication of the Archdiocese of Los Angeles, California. He is the father of three children and the grandfather of three. He resides in rural Huntington, Indiana. ❖

Linda Scher Leist resides in Huntington with her husband of 48 years. They are the parents of six children and the grandparents of eight. Even before her birth, she was blessed to have a relationship with Blessed Father Solanus Casey, O.F.M. Cap. When she was just a young girl, her gramma told her that her mother was planning to abort her soon after she discovered the presence of the unborn child within her. The timing wasn't good for her. However, Linda's maternal grandparents convinced her mother to first seek the counsel of a new priest in Huntington, Father Solanus Casey. Many favors and miracles were being reported as a result of his holy intercessions. So her mother agreed to see him, and in his gentle, loving way he convinced Linda's mother to let her live. She is very grateful for the intercession of this holy, gentle priest, whom she already considers to be a saint. He saved her life as a tiny unborn child, and she believes that he is still interceding for herself, family, and friends, as many blessings, miracles, and favors are still being reported, due to the intercession of Blessed Solanus Casey. Deo Gratias! ❖

Printed in the USA
CPSIA information can be obtained
at www.ICGtesting.com
LVHW050622081224
798393LV00018B/246